The Onesimos Nesib Seminary in Aira, Western Ethiopia

The Beginning

Ernst Bauerochse

AF201397

Ernst Bauerochse

The Onesimos Nesib Seminary

in Aira, Western Ethiopia

–

The Beginning

Bibliografische Information der Deutschen Nationalbibliothek:

Die Deutsche Nationalbibliothek verzeichnet diese Publikation in der Deutschen Nationalbibliografie. Detaillierte bibliografische Daten sind im Internet über dnb.dnb.de abrufbar.

© 2017 Ernst Bauerochse

Herstellung und Verlag: BoD – Books on Demand, Norderstedt

Titelfoto: Dank an Dietrich Wassmann, sen., Hermannsburg

Alle anderen Fotos: Ernst Bauerochse

ISBN: 978-3-7460-3334-1

The Evangelist Course in Calliya Eekkaa in October, 1954.................6

The first Evangelists employed by the Evangelical Congregations...12

More Evangelists Courses and Monthly Meetings..........................14

A Bible School must be built!...15

The Participants of the First Course 1961-1963.............................19

A Crash Course for Pastors..22

The Participants of the Second Course...25

Bidding Farewell...28

The Evangelist Course in Calliya Eekkaa in October, 1954

In March 1954[1], the Reverend Hinrich Rathje and myself were given permission by the Ethiopian Government, to come to Ethiopia to work there as missionaries. Together with my wife Brunhilde and our little boy Hartmut, I left Germany on May 10, and we arrived at the mission station of Airs in Western Ethiopia on June 12, 1954. At that time, the German Hermannsburg Mission, to which we belonged, had only one station left from the three which she had before the Italian invasion. That was Aira. The stations at Addis Ababa and Buunoo Beddellee had been lost in the course of the Italian invasion and the Second World War.

In August 1954, a meeting of Church Elders from the 17 congregations situated around Aira and Challiya was held at Aira. They urgently asked for theological training of the volunteer preachers who carried the main burden of the Sunday worship services. Most of them had never received any formal training for preaching. At that time, there were only three local pastors, Luba (Pastor) Dafaa Jammoo, President of the Evangelical Congregations in Gimbii Awraja, Luba Taasisaa Dureessaa, Headmaster of the Mission School at Aira, and Luba Ashanaa Naggaadee in Calliya Eekkaa. So, it was clear that a training course for the voluntary preachers was urgently needed. A suitable time seemed to be from October 4 to 22, 1954, and Calliya Eekkaa was the most convenient place for it, as most participants were able to reach Eekkaa from their homes in the morning, and to return home in the afternoon. For the preachers living at Aira, Buyyee and Maasina'o a smaller course could be arranged at Aira.

Rev. Rathje and myself prepared a time table. I should teach Old and New Testament and in addition Church History, Rathje was to

---

[1]   Dates mentioned in this report follow the Western calendar

take practical subjects like preaching and spiritual care in the congregations. Both of us needed an interpreter, and Pastor Dafaa was ready to do that for us.

The attendance of the course was overwhelming. I asked Pastor Dafaa to prepare a list with the names of all participants, and also their daily attendance. I have kept this list since 1954. It seems to me to be very important for the history of the evangelical congregations in the Gimbii District. I attach it therefore to this report. At that time, all official papers were written in Amharic. Pastor Dafaa has written the following headline at the top of the list in Amharic language, as was the custom at that time:

> *Bä Calliya Eekkaa lay yätädärägäw ye Wangelawuyaan Masiltägna*
>
> *Mäskäräm 24 qän iskä Tikimt 12/47 A. M.*

As many participants came from Eekkaa and Gaala'o, he has listed these two congregations first. We first conducted a small course for preachers from Aira, Buuyee and Maasina'o at Aira, which was more convenient for them than going to Eekkaa. Therefore, they were not listed among the attendants of the larger course at Calliya Eekkaa.

I should mention that in September 1954, I had been invited to preach at Mandi during a Bible Week. I was guest in the house of Rev. Arne Hansson from the Swedish Evangelical Mission who had started a Bible School in Mandii. As he had only small funds for the running of the School, he had requested the congregations to give assistance to the students sent by them. But this had worked only for a short time. Several students had to leave, because they did not get regular support from their congregations, so the effect of the teaching was small. What I saw in Mandii gave me the idea of founding a bible school at Aira as soon as possible, and supply the necessary funds for the support of the students from the Mission. This way, I could expect that the students would concentrate on the teaching and not interrupt their study.

I now list the names of those who attended the 1954 Evangelist Course at Eekkaa.

From Eekkaa:

1. Dheeressaa Reebuu, 2. Olaanaa Galataa, 3. Jaalal Naggaadee, 4. Lamuu Shobor, 5. Cawaaqaa Waayyuu, 6. Tafaraa Buushan, 7. Abara Teessoo, 8. Taayee Bayanaa, 9. Tarreesaa Tuuchoo, 10. Disaasaa Xooshaa, 11. Gammadaa Akkayyuu, 12. Ragaasaa Buushan, 13. Jogoraa Nagawoo, 14. Oljirraa Tirsuu, 15. Umataa Aagaa, 16. Bayyissaa Tuuchoo, 17. Fidaa Tolasaa, 18. Ummataa Danoo, 19. Taasisaa Shobor, 20. Dhugumaa Jigsaa, 21. Dheereessaa Lamuu, 22. Nagaasaa Lamuu, 23. Dagaagoo Ashanaa, 24. Darasuu Qixxeesaa, 25. Baatuu Nagawoo, 26. Disaasaa Amantee, 27. Tarrafaa Reebuu, 28. Tafarii Daannoo, 29. Likaasaa Urgeessaa, 30. Nagarii Coophee, 31. Olii Mijanaa, 32. Dhinaa Gammachuu, 33. Tarrafaa Asuudaa, 34. Taafasa Barkii, 35. Abdiisaa Bagoosaa.

From Gaalawoo:

1. Ciibsaa Baacaa, 2. Hambisaa Tooboo, 3. Kumarraa Dhaabaa, 4. Dagafaa Lammii, 5. Oljiraa Tufaa, 6. Ayyaanaa Ligdii, 7. Hirphaa Dinqaa, 8. Makonnen Ciibsaa, 9. Makonnen Raggaasaa, 10. Itaanaa Geetaa, 11. Raagaa Shuumii, 12. Wadaajoo Baalchaa, 13. Oljiraa Dhaabaa, 14. Gammadaa Fayyisaa, 15. Olaanaa Waaqjiraa, 16. Oljiraa Bushuraa, 17. Olaanaa Dhowwaa, 18. Qaadiidaa Giddii, 19. Barkeesaa Lamuu, 20. Itaanaa Ammayaa, 21. Hundeesaa Fayyisaa, 22. Itafaa Baacaa, 23. Hirphaa Shuumii, 24. Faradaa Garbaa, 25. Itaanaa Baaboo, 26. Gabbisaa Atoomsaa, 27. Galalchaa Tum'ee, 28. Makonnen Baacaa, 29. Dheeressaa Baacaa, 30. Umataa Inseenee, 31. Dhugumaa Dootii, 32. Danuu Inaashee, 33. Worqina

Waadaajoo, 34. Addisuu Gobbuu, 35. Tarrafuu Garbaabaa, 36. Itafaa Diimee, 37. Danuu Iguu, 38. Idoosaa Farajaa, 39. Shifärawu Geetaa, 40. Mardaasaa Seedaa, 41. Gobanaa Wacoo, 42. Oliiqaa Wayyeessaa.

From Kormee:

1. Galataa Hirphoo, 2. Imaanaa Reebuu, 3. Nagasa Dotii, 4. Waayyeessaa Hirphoo, 5. Tarfaasaa Galataa, 6. Bulii Kuusaa, 7.Miijanaa Qannoo, 8. Tareessaa Raaree, 9. Tasammaa Dhabsuu, 10. Dhugaasaa Qixxeessaa, 11. Tasammaa Shooroo.

From Guduruu:

1. Bantii Gammachuu, 2. Gaaromaa Galatee, 3. Taafasa Ngarii, 5. Wulii Nagoo, 6. Tarfaasaa Moosaa, 7.Kanarraa Galatee, 8. Hundee Waacoo.

From Maasina'o:

1. Itaanaa Abakuu, 2. Ayyaanaa Tooboo, 3. Namarraa Silgaa, 4. Fufaa Boojjii, 5. Baqqaanaa Abakuu.

From Kusaa'ee:

1. Gorbaa Tirsuu, 2. Gobbuu Boongaa, 3. Caalaa Tirsuu, 4. Kumaraa Lammeessaa, 5. Bokkoree Jootee.

From Loomaa:

1. Bayyisaa Dhaabaa, 2. Gurmeessaa Beeraa, 3. Waaqwayyaa Magarsaa, 4. Dhufeeraa Mulataa, 5. Tiksaa Daaqaa.

From Dargee:

1. Dhibbisaa Waaqwayyaa, 2. Karorsaa Dhinsaa.

From Baaboo Dambii:

1. Kumarraa Lamuu, 2. Asafaa Sirnaa, 3. Ganatii Dhaabaa

(?), 4. Cirachoo Yaadataa, 5. Abdiisaa Fufaa, 6. Ummataa Bulii, 7. Itaanaa Waaqoo, 8. Ummataa Ujukkaa (?), 9. Birhanuu, Ootaa, 10. Sanbataa Gonjee.

From Waatoo:

1. Ragaasaa Galataa, 2. Godanaa Yaraa, 3. Jaallataa Abdii, 4. Guddaatoo Abdii, 5. Hailu Tooboo, 6. Rundaasaa Gasharaa.

From Inamaayi Kobbaraa:

1. Ayyaanaa Bultum, 2. Barii Kuusaa, 3. Qannoo Ilikee, 4. Biraasaa Dhufeeraa, 5. Xirkanaa Gammadaa, 6. Täsämaa Barkeessaa.

From Jaarsoo Baddeessoo:

1. Bulii Gooroo, 2. Amanuu Gaasaa.

From Teegii:

1. Nagarii Tumtuu, 2. Nagarii Gobbuu, 3. Hata'uu Aagaa, 4. Tasammaa Fayyissaa, 5. Birhanuu Bakakkoo, 6. Fufaa Booboo, 7. Darasuu Bakakkoo.

From Daannoo:

1. Nagaasaa Tolaa, 2. Tarrrafaa Galatee, 3. Waaqjiraa Odaa, 4. Dhinaa Garbaa, 5. Galataa Bakaree, 6. Taasisaa Dotii, 7. Teesoo Bagoosaa.

From Inaangoo Kobbaraa:

1. Ayyalewu Fufaa

From Waayyuu Manii:

1. Raggaasaa Jaatee, 2. Ayyaanaa Takkatuu, 3. Bantii Gaantii, 4. Makonnin Dhibbisaa.

From Jaarsoo Gaalawoo:

1. Olaanaa Dhinsaa, 2. Adinawu Baguu, 3. Umataa

Abbaamagal, 4. Tafaraa Biduu, 5. Sanbataa Milkii.

This list contains the names of 161 attendants coming from 17 congregations. The course at Aira was much smaller. Unfortunately, I have not taken down the names of the attendants. There were about six or seven. So, altogether one can say that almost 170 voluntary preachers from about twenty congregations received some training in the autumn of 1954.

In letters which I received from my former student Rev. Tafaraa Falaasaa in 2006 and again in 2013, he emphasized three facts: „1. At the beginning, it was very difficult to find a Holy Bible or New Testament. 2. The voluntary preachers elected were mainly those who had learned the Ethiopian alphabet (haa, huu, hii etc.) in Ethiopian letters in their houses without any teachers. 3. Among the voluntary preachers were some women who at that time did not participate in the evangelist course." He mentions Birqii Abakuu from Maasina'o and Yeshimabet Gobbuu, the wife of the evangelist Waaqwayyaa Dhufeeraa from Aira.

For me, the courses in Calliya Eekkaa provided an encouraging and important experience. I realized that the real missionaries to the people of Western Wallagga were not the ordained missionaries from Germany, but the local preachers who were far better qualified both to preach the Gospel in the existing congregations, as well as to go to new areas and evangelize people there. The local pastors which I mentioned were hardly able to go into new areas. Pastor Dafaa was bothered by many court cases which had been opened against evangelical believers. They were accused of conducting prayer meetings illegally either in their private houses, or in the so-called „Prayer Houses" (Mana Tsalotii, Tselot Bet, as the churches of the evangelical believers were called). It was argued that worship services should only be held in Orthodox churches or by permission of the Orthodox bishop. Therefore, Pastor Dafaa often had to travel to Gimbii, the district town, or to Naqamtee, the provincial capital, or even to Addis Ababa to attend court cases.

Pastor Taasisaa was Head Master of the mission school and therefore had to stay in Aira, and Pastor Ashanaa Naggaadee had a lot of work in the big congregation of Eekkaa. So, the potential to carry the gospel into new areas stayed with the voluntary preachers. I tried as much as possible to devote my time and energy to their training. This was not easy, for in those early years of my stay at Aira, we had neither a Bible School nor accommodations for teaching or for the housing of students. I myself was burdened with a lot of building and administrative work on the station. Nevertheless, apart from Sunday preaching commitments and the teaching of confirmation classes in several congregations, I kept the training of local evangelists as an important task in my mind.

The first Evangelists employed by the Evangelical Congregations

Mission Conventions, in German: "Missionsfeste", played a great role in the history of the German Hermannsburg Mission in Germany since 1851. The two Hermannsburg missionaries who had been permitted in 1951 by the Imperial Ethiopian Government to return to Ethiopia, Rev. Dietrich Wassmann sen. and Hermann Hornbostel, thought that such gatherings would also be useful and encouraging in Wallagga. They planned the first „Sibsaba Wangeelaa" (Gospel Convention), as it was called by the local Christians, for January, 1954. It was held on the Mission Station at Aira. Unfortunately, Rev. Wassmann died the same month in Addis Ababa.

A collection was made, and the money given was used to employ two evangelists. One of them was Itaanaa Getaa from Gaalawo. The other was from Eekkaa, but his name has slipped my memory. As the congregations had to raise the money for the salary of Pastor Dafaa and Pastor Ashanaa (Pastor Taasisaa received his salary from the Mission), the idea was to employ two evangelists with a very small salary taken from the collection of the Gospel Meeting. But this could only be done as long as the collection money lasted. The next Gospel Convention was held in December, 1954, at Calliya Eekkaa. The amount of money given was bigger than that of January, 1954, and four evangelists were employed, all of them from Eekkaa. Their names were Abbosee Dinqaa, Darasuu Qixeesaa, Gammadaa Akkayyuu, and Nagaasaa Lamuu. There were especially two areas in which they worked, the Kobbaraa District, and the Ganjii District north and east of Aira.

On Sunday, January 1 1956, I had to conduct a worship service in the congregation of Inamaayi Kobbaraa. It was a long ride of about eight hours from Aira. After the worship service, I was invited by the "Father" of the congregation (the church had been built on his land) Gammadaa Deentaa. When I left, some men from the congregation accompanied me for some time. They complained that up to that time, no confirmation teaching had been held in Inamaayi Kobbaraa, and one of them said in the Oromo language: "Abdii keenya kutannee," in English: „We have cut off our hope." Instantly I replied: "Abdii keessani hin kutatina!" - „Do not cut off your hope!" It became clear to me that something had to be done to arrange for confirmation classes in the four congregations of the Koobbaraa District: Inamaayi Kobbaraa, Inaango Kobbaraa, Allee Kobbaraa, and Bukee Kobbaraa.

But who should go there? Because of the distance and the bad roads, I could not go there to teach. Neither could one of the pastors do that. The only people who could be entrusted with the teaching of confirmation classes in these congregations, were the four evangelists from Eekaa. But up to that time they had not been trained for such a task. They had, of course, been confirmed, but to teach confirmation classes demanded more. I told Pastor Dafaa, that I would call the four evangelists to Aira, give them guidance on how to teach confirmation classes, and then send them to the Kobbaraa District. Pastor Dafaa wholeheartedly agreed.

It was clear that this could only be a small beginning. I was responsible for the work at the Aira station and was burdened by a lot of work. Therefore, I could give the four evangelists only a short introduction in teaching the first part of Luther's Small Catechism on the Ten Commandments. With this, they had to start to show the congregations that we were serious in providing confirmation teaching. I planned to call the evangelists again to give them more instructions on the other parts of Luther's Catechism. When I had to conduct a Sunday worship service at Inaangoo Koobbaraa in September 1956, I met Nagaasaa Lamuu there. He helped me to register more than thirty children for baptism. Exactly one month later, I broke my leg, had to be in bed for six weeks and then fly to Addis Ababa where my leg had to be operated on. This kept me out of work for months. In the meantime, the evangelists had continued the teaching as best as they could, and many believers could be confirmed.

More Evangelists Courses and Monthly Meetings

The good experience of the Evangelist Course of 1954 led us to plan another course by the end of September, 1955. But I had two problems: Rev. Rathje was no longer in Aira. For reasons of bad health, he had gone back to Germany. The second problem was that Pastor Dafaa was not in Aira. Once more, he had to attend a court case at the district town of Gimbii, where evangelical Christians had been accused and were in danger of being imprisoned. I was not yet firm enough in the Oromo language to conduct the course all by myself. So, I asked Pastor Taasisaa to come with me to Eekkaa. He spoke sufficient English to translate my teaching into Oromiffa. But he could only stay for two days. The third day, he had to return to Aira for the opening of the school. I tried to teach alone in the Oromo language, but when, by 4 o'clock in the afternoon, I had to send the participants home and Pastor

Dafaa had not arrived, I decided to propose that in future we meet every month on the first Monday. This was accepted, and it became a regular feature of the work, not only in Calliya, but also in Aira, and later on in other places.

A Bible School must be built!

In 1958, two representatives of the Hermannsburg Mission Board visited us. We showed them around in a number of congregations and discussed with them the challenges and problems of our work. One such problem was the supply of drinking water on the station. There were some complaints that not enough water was supplied for the hospital and for the school. So, the visitors from Germany asked us: "Where do you put your priorities?" I thought, now it was time for me to present to them my priorities, and I said: "I have been here at Aira now for four years, but honestly speaking, most of my time has been spent in building work, administration and travelling around. But I have been trained and sent out to preach the Gospel, and what we need most of all is a bible school. That is my priority." I went as far as saying: „I am due to go on home leave next year, and if during that time no bible school is built, I shall not come to Ethiopia again."

This obviously made a great impression on our visitors from the Home Board, and from Hermannsburg the order was given to build a bible school without delay. When I returned to Aira in September 1960 after my home leave, the bible school building was almost ready to be occupied. It consisted of two buildings in the simple wood and clay style which we were using throughout the station. One building was intended for two classrooms, a library and an office, the other one was to be the boarding house for 20 students. The houses had corrugated iron roofs.

The initial buildings of the Onesimos Nesib Bible School situated at a small distance from the Aira Mission Station

Now, it was time to prepare for the teaching. Most of all, the students had to be elected. I left this to the congregations and the pastors' conference of our district. They knew best which young men from their midst would be most qualified for the training and for later service in the church. I had to prepare the lessons I would have to give. This was not easy. I enjoyed teaching and preparing it, but at the same time, there were so many other challenges and problems in the mission as well as in the congregations which I had to deal with as Field Director, Treasurer of the Mission and of the congregations and advisor to the Church President. Every Sunday, I had to preach in another congregation. There were meetings of the Gimbii Board not only in Aira, but also in Najjoo and Mandii. I worked on a new liturgy for the worship services, not only for pastors, but also for evangelists. Liturgies for baptism, confirmation, burial and other church events had to follow. We re-worded the Oromo version of the Apostolic Creed and the Ten Commandments. In June 1961, I was finally ready to start with a first short course in the Bible School, but this was not yet for evangelists, but for church secretaries who should keep registers on church membership,

16

baptisms, burials, etc. Two more such courses followed in July 1961.

On October 2, 1961, all preparations were ready to start with the Bible School teaching. 20 students arrived for the first evangelist course. Unfortunately, I have not kept a list of this group. I had hoped to put down all these events, the names of the students, the teaching subjects, and all our experiences in the Bible School in a book, and I had even bought a suitable book in Addis Ababa. But, alas! I never found the time to do that. Now, when I write this report, 56 years have elapsed since we opened the Onesimos Nesib Bible School, as I named it, and as in the meantime I had to divert my work and thinking to so many different subjects - as Director of a Radio Station and later as Head of a Department in the Evangelical Lutheran Mission in Lower Saxony, Germany, I am no longer able to list the names of all students. But one of them, Tafarraa Falaasaa, helped me greatly. He was from Maasinao, not far from Aira. After the completion of the first course, he helped in the administration of the local synod of the church and in the running of the Bible School. After my departure from Aira in December, 1964, he became pastor and superintendent in the Church. With his help, I have I been able to put together the names of the students. The following photo shows him around the year 2000.

Luba Tafarraa Falaasaa, Bible School student 1961 to 1963. Photo taken around 2000

I had planned the training for two years (4 semesters). For the second course which started on October 1, 1963, I changed it to 2 1/2 years (5 semesters). Fortunately, I was not the only teacher. By chance, I got a helper in Petros Cawaaqaa from Naqamte. He had been trained by the Swedish Evangelical

Mission (SEM) at Aduwa, and had been employed for the SEM school in Najjoo. But he and another young teacher had an argument with the Swedish Missionary at Najjoo, Rev. Bertil Andreasson, and came to Aira to look for work. I told them that we would have work for them, but they would first have to go back to Najjoo, be reconciled with Rev. Andreasson and bring me a written statement from him that he had no objection if we employ them. They did so, and I employed Petros as teacher for Amharic and other secular subjects in the Bible School.

I had hoped to get help in teaching from the local pastors Dafaa and Taasisaa. But as they were so heavily engaged in the congregational and educational work, they could help me only very little. Later, younger pastors like Olaanaa Lamuu from Aira and Ayellew Rooroo from Kormee helped me. When it came to name the Bible School, I had decided to call it the Onesimos Nesib Bible School. The most important tools in our congregational work was the Bible as translated by Onesimos Nesib, and also the hymnbook he had compiled. It contained Luther's catechism (though in a form slightly different from the one used in Germany) and a short order of worship. Both proved to be helpful in bringing many Oromos to faith in Christ. I considered Onesimos' work quite exceptional and most important for the mission work. That was the reason why I gave the Bible School the name Onesimos Nesib Bible School.

As to the subjects we taught, I have mentioned that Petros taught Amharic and some other subjects of general education. I myself taught the exegesis of Old and New Testament books, Church History, History and Doctrine of the different Christian confessions including the Orthodox churches, and similar subjects. Occasionally, Pastor Dafaa would tell students of events and developments in the Church. Of course, morning and evening devotions, prayers and the singing of hymns and psalms were also part of our daily work. As much as possible, the students would take on preaching assignments in the congregations on Sundays. Also Petros, who was born in a Muslim family in Naqamte and had been converted when he attended the mission school there, would preach in the Aira church.

The Participants of the First Course 1961-1963

Pastor Tafarraa Falaasaa has sent me the following list of the first course:

From Calliya Eekkaa:

Aabbosee Dinqaa

Darasuu Qixxeesaa

Gammadaa Akkayyuu

Nagaasaa Lamu

Dagaagoo Ashanaa

From Gaala'o:

Dheeressaa Bacaa

Hambisaa Tooboo

Raagaa Shuumii

From Aira:

Ayyaanaa Shawl

Guutaa Raassoo (Somboo)

Tafarraa Falaasaa (Maassina'o)

Yigezu Amante

From Ganjii:

Hambisaa Tutji (Ganjii Deembii)

Itaffaa Alabee (Ganjii Dongoro)

From Guduruu:

 Taafassa Nagarii

From Gutee Likaasaa:

 Hundeesaa Dinpaa

 Hundeesaa Likaasaa

 Likaasaa Yaadasaa

From Koobbaraa:

 Dibisaa Ayyaanaa

From Kormee:

 Tasammaa Dhabsuu

From Waatoo:

 Jabeessaa Dinqaa

These are 21 names. Tafarraa Falaasaa mentions four students who did not stay for the full course. He writes:

 Ayyaana Shawl from Aira: "He stopped in between,

 Hundeesaa Dinqaa from Gutee Likaasaa: "stopped in between,"

 Raggaasaa Jobir from Aira: "Former Orthodox priest. Incomplete", and

 Likaasa Yaadasaa from Gutee Likaasaa. "Incomplete".

I had originally planned for 20 students. It could be that, for some time, we had more than 20 students.

As to Ragaasaa Jobir, former Orthodox priest from Aira, he is shown on the photo showing the members of the second Bible School course (see below). Another Orthodox priest, Qadjeelaa Jaawii from Gaala'o, for some time attended a pastors course at Najjoo (1956/57) and later the Bible School at Aira.

From left: Hundeesaa Dinqaa, Dibisaa Ayyaanaa, Ayyaanaa Shawl, Dagaagoo Ashanaa, Gammadaa Akkayyuu, Tafaraa Falaasaa, Jabeessaa Dinqaa, Itafaa Alabee, Yigezu Amantee, Hambisaa Tutji, Taafassa Nagari, Hambisaa Tooboo, Aabbosee Dinqaa, Tasammaa Dhabsuu, Dheeressaa Bacaa

From left: Guutaa Raassoo, Ernst Bauerochse, in the last row: Olaanaa Waaqjiraa (member of the crash course for pastors, see below), Dheeressaa Baacaa and Gammadaa Akkayyuu, then Nagaasaa Lamuu. Taafaaa Nagarii and Dagaagoo Ashanaa

A Crash Course for Pastors

In 1962, Pastor Dafaa, President of the Wallagga Synode, came to me and said, the need for future pastors is so great that you must conduct a special crash course for some men who have proved to be reliable and dedicated workers in the church, and who are gifted to do the work of a pastor. The Church leaders had selected Aabbosee Dinqaa from the Bible School students and added Olaanaa Waaqjiraa from Gaala'o, up to then assistant in the Eekkaa clinic, and Tolaasaa Hundee, teacher in the Aira Mission School. From the area of the Swedish Mission north of Aira, four men were sent. They were:

> Kitila Danuu from Boojii,
>
> Waddajoo Xabaluu from Nadjoo,
>
> Tagenye Daankii from Mandii and
>
> Olaanaa Nagarii, also from Mandii.

The congregation of Naqamte of the Central Synod of the Mekane

Yesus Church sent Raggaasaa Badhaadhaa. I had only a few months to teach these men. That was a heavy burden which we could hardly shoulder. But we did all we could to enable these men to do pastoral work in the church. The plan was that they should get more training later on.

In December 1962, the President of the Ethiopian Evangelical Church Mekane Yesus, Ato (later: Dr.) Emanuel Gabre Sellasie, and the then advisor to the Church, Manfred Lundgren from Sweden, visited us. The Synod resolved that the three members of the pastors course from Aira and Calliya, Aabbosee Dinqaa, Olaanaa Waaqjiraa, and Tolasaa Hundee, should be examined in the presence of the visitors and be ordained deacons on Sunday, December 16, 1962. Three months later, on Ethiopian Easter Monday, March 3, 1963, they were ordained pastors. The participants from Bojji, Najjoo, and Mandii, continued until the end of the evangelist course in early July 1963 and were ordained in Mandii on August 4, 1963 during a meeting of all pastors of the Synod.

During the last week of June 1963, all students had to write an examination paper and a sermon. In the first week of July, oral examinations were held. The result was that all students who had stayed until the end of the course, passed with good results and could be employed as evangelists by the congregations. This was a great step forward in the spiritual care for the congregations in the Wallagga Synod.

On Sunday, December 16, 1962, three members of the Pastors Crash Course were ordained by President Pastor Dafaa Jammoo in Aira. The photo taken after the Ordination Service shows, from left: Pastor Ashanaa Naggaadee from Calliya Eekkaa, Pastor Taasisaa Dureessa from Aira. In white talars only: Tolaasaa Hundee, Aabbosee Dinqaa and Olaanaa Waaqjiraa. In the back: Rev. Ernst Bauerochse and Rev. Erwin Meyer (Calliyaa). Right with hat: Ato Emmanuel Gebre Sellasee, Addis Ababa. Kneeling in front: Rev. Manfred Lundgren and President Pastor Dafaa Jammoo.

As to Raggaasaa Badhaadhaa, he went back to Naqamte to serve the congregation which had sent him. He was ordained pastor in the Mekane Yesus congregation in Addis Abeba together with Esra Gebre Medhin who at that time was General Secretary of the Church, on Sunday, March 1, 1964. Ragaggaasaa studied in the Mekane Yesus Seminary in Addis Ababa and later became pastor of the congregation in the town of Bushooftuu/Debre Zeit southwest of Addis Ababa. He did an excellent job especially during the Derg dictatorship. For me, it was most remarkable that he came from a Qaalluu Family. Qaalluus were something like priests of the old Oromo religion.

Tafarraa Falaasaa mentions a certain Getacho Gensato from

Kambata. But he has come to the Onesiomos Nesib Bible School later. When I visited Hosaina in Kambata in 1988, I was addressed by a pastor who told me that he had got his training in the Bible School in Aira when Rev. Jürgen Wesenick headed the school. That must have been after 1966.

From left: Pastor Kitila Danuu, Pastor Waaddajoo Xabaluu, Pastor Tagenye Daankii and Pastor Olaanaa Nagarii on the day of their ordination in Mandii, Sunday, August 4, 1963, together with Rev. Ernst Bauerochse

The Participants of the Second Course

In spite of the high demands which the growing work in the Mission as well as in the Synod put on us, it was clear that we would continue teaching another evangelist course in the Bible School. Again, students were elected by the congregation elders and the Synod pastors. Tafarraa Falaasaa has supplied me with the names of the participants as much as he could find out. In a letter of October 2, 2009, he writes: "But it is not so easy to find the names of the 2nd course correctly. But I tried to ask the participants of that course as much as possible." I am very grateful to Tafarraa Falaasaa for the effort he has put in the compilation of this list - almost 60 years after the course was held, a course in which Taffaraa himself did not participate. He lists the following names:

>Abbaraa Naadoo from Jaarsoo Daalatii (murdered in Boojji during the Derg regime)
>
>Birhanu Ootaa from Baaboo Dambii
>
>Ciibsaa Baacaa from Gaala'o
>
>Dinqaa Qannoo from Korme
>
>Haylu Tarfaasaa from Allee Koobbaraa
>
>Itaanaa Geta from Gaal'ao
>
>Jimmaataa Tarreesaa from Aira
>
>Makonnen Baacaa from Gaal'ao
>
>Makonnen Ciibsaa from Calliya
>
>Mijannaa Qannoo from Korme
>
>Oli Miijanaa from Calliya Eekkaa
>
>Raggaasaa Jobir from Aira
>
>Soboqaa Diillaa from Mandii
>
>Taafasaa Barkii from Calliya
>
>Tafaraa Darasuu from Buunoo Beddellee
>
>Waaqjiraa Dheereessaa from Aira
>
>Waaqjiraa Ganatii from Gullisoo
>
>Waaqwayyaa Dhufeeraa from Aira
>
>Yaadasaa Riqituu from Calliya

Tafarraa Falaasaa named two more students: Jallataa Nagarii from

Boojii and Solomon Dina from Gaala'o. But Tasgaraa Hirphoo, later President of the West Wallagga Synod, affirms that these two were not members of the second course, but of a later one.

Bidding Farewell

Unfortunately, I could not stay in Aira until the end of the second course. For my family, the time was up for a second home leave. Especially my wife who was pregnant, needed hospital treatment in Germany. So, I had to hand over the responsibility for the Onesimos Nesib Bible School to the Reverend Johannes Launhardt who had been working in Addis Ababa until that time and now moved to Aira together with his family. So, my engagement in the work of the Onesimos Nesib Bible School ended in December, 1964. All students gave me a moving farewell at our little airport, when on December 4, we boarded the small plane of the Missionary Aviation Fellowship, which took us to Goree, from where we reached Addis Ababa on the same day. On December 13, 1964, we flew to Germany.

Rev. Ernst Bauerochse bidding farewell to Pastor Ayyelew Rooroo, who also taught at the Onesimos Nesib Bible School, and students. Last in the row (on left): Tafaraa Falaasaa.

For my wife, a long stay in hospital followed, but we could return to Ethiopia in September, 1965. New assignments waited for me in the Church and in the Mission in Addis Ababa. I must therefore leave it to others to write about the development of the Onesimos Nesib Bible School, as Pastor Tafaraa Falaasaa has already done. Later, the Bible School was upgraded to be a theological seminary, and thereby was enabled even better to carry out the important task for which it had been opened in 1961.

It so happened that I visited Aira in 1966 when the second course was about to end. I took a photo, but I did not notice the names.

Students of the second course (1963 to 1966) in front of the Onesimos Nesib Bible School

Years later, in 1988, I had the chance to teach there again. But a severe malaria infection forced me to return to Germany.

May God bless all those who now teach and learn in the Onesimos Nesib Seminary!

In August, 2017

Ernst Bauerochse

Also by Ernst Bauerochse:

A Vision Finds Fulfillment. Hermannsburg Mission in Ethiopia.

LIT Verlag, Fresnostr. 2, D-48159 Münster, Germany

Berlin, Zürich 2008

ISBN 978-3-8258-9880-9 / 978-3-03735-939-6

Distributed in the UK by Global Book Marketing, 99B Wallis Rd., London, E9 5LN

This book tells the story of the work of four missionaries and their successors which led to the establishment of the Ethiopian Evangelical Church - Mekane Yesus. The author draws from documents in the archives in Hermannsburg and his own experience working in Ethiopia from 1954 to 1974.